A GATHERING OF GRACE

A SERVICE FOR HOLY WEEK

BY DOUGLAS NOLAN · ORCHESTRATED BY BRAD NIX

① This symbol indicates a track number on the StudioTrax CD or SplitTrax CD.

Duration: ca. 37 Minutes

ISBN 9-781-5400-4013-8

SHAWNEE ✿ PRESS

EXCLUSIVELY DISTRIBUTED BY

7777 W. BLUEMOUND RD. P.O. BOX 13819 MILWAUKEE, WI 53213

Visit Hal Leonard Online at
www.halleonard.com

Visit Shawnee Press Online at
www.shawneepress.com

Contact us:
Hal Leonard
7777 West Bluemound Road
Milwaukee, WI 53213
Email: info@halleonard.com

In Europe, contact:
Hal Leonard Europe Limited
Distribution Centre, Newmarket Road
Bury St Edmunds, Suffolk, IP33 3YB
Email: info@halleonardeurope.com

In Australia, contact:
Hal Leonard Australia Pty. Ltd.
4 Lentara Court
Cheltenham, Victoria, 3192 Australia
Email: info@halleonard.com.au

FOREWORD

In the serenity of this sacred place, let us pause and recall the life, ministry, and passion of Jesus. Let us consider His journey of grace and embrace His gospel of peace. Through the assurance of scripture, the promise of prayer, and the encouragement of music, we will still our hearts and remember. As we listen and learn, may we breathe in the healing love that is God's Spirit of truth. May we draw closer to the cross and abide in its shadow. In this gathering of grace, may we, as one people, worship in hope and cast our dreams to the coming of dawn.

PERFORMANCE NOTES

This cantata is structured to be freely adapted to fit the traditions and rituals of your congregation. This work could be enhanced with sacred symbols, banners, or presented progressively throughout the Lenten or Holy Week observances. The lighting and extinguishing of candles would certainly be one possibility with the work. It may also be expanded to include a pastoral devotion or homily, the celebration of communion, hymn singing, and prayers.

A GATHERING OF GRACE
Prelude of Shadows

Music by
DOUGLAS NOLAN (BMI)

ACCOMP.

6

NARRATION:
We gather today to consider the life and ministry of Jesus. In the quiet of this sacred place, we give our hearts to hope and reflect upon our own need for a Savior. In the assurance of scripture, the promise of prayer, and the encouragement of song, we will rest and remember. In this deep remembrance, may we embrace the grace gift that is ours through Jesus Christ, our Lord.

PRAYER:
God of the still, small voice, breath into us Your perfect peace and quiet our spirit. Sing gently into our hearts Your music of grace. May we listen, and learn to become Your instruments of truth in a troubled world. May we follow You in faith and share Your journey of service and sacrifice. Help us walk this trail of tears clinging to Your assurance and the promise of Your presence. We pray this in the name of the One who said, "I AM THE WAY…THE TRUTH…AND THE LIFE." *(John 14:6 KJV)*

dedicated to Clyde Everett Kidd in honor of his thirty-six years of enthusiastic and exceptional service as
Director of the Chancel Choir, First United Methodist Church, Sacramento, CA
commissioned with much love and appreciation by the congregation

IN THE STILLNESS OF THIS MOMENT

Words by
JOSEPH M. MARTIN (BMI)

Music by
JOSEPH M. MARTIN
and DAVID ANGERMAN (ASCAP)
Arranged by
DOUGLAS NOLAN (BMI)

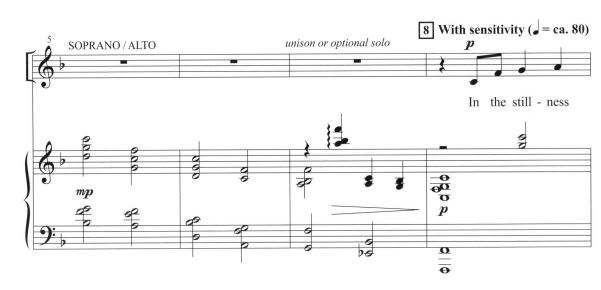

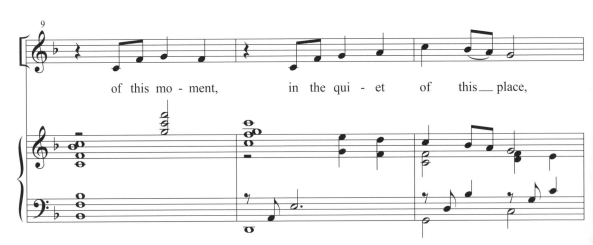

hope of glo-ry and we hold the gift of love._____

How mar-vel-ous! How won-der-ful!

Oh, how mar-vel-ous! Oh, how won-der-ful!

And my song shall ev-er be._____

* Tune: MY SAVIOR'S LOVE, Charles H. Gabriel, 1856-1932
Words: Charles H. Gabriel

A GATHERING OF GRACE - SA(T)B

of this mo - ment, as we calm our hearts and __ minds, __

we feel Your ten - der mer - cy and the gift of

peace di - vine. As we gath - er now to wor - ship,

let us find a place of rest,

where the gifts of Word and mu - sic

feed our souls with heav-en's best.

14

our sur - ren - der are an off - 'ring made of __ praise.

For the won - der of sal - va - tion, is a mir - a - cle of

grace. How mar - vel - ous! Oh, how mar - vel - ous!

Slowly, freely (♩ = ca. 69)

NARRATION:
The scriptures tell us that Jesus went through all the towns and villages teaching the good news of the kingdom and healing every disease and affliction. When He saw the crowds, He was filled with compassion because they were hopeless and lost, like a sheep without a shepherd. Longing to reach them, He began to lead them, "For everyone who asks receives; the one who seeks will surely find and to everyone who knocks, the door will be opened." *(Matthew 9:35; 7:8 paraphrased)*

ASK OF ME

Words by
MARY FOIL

Music by
DOUGLAS NOLAN (BMI)

Ask of Me, and I will hear.

Ask of Me, for I am near. I will hear the

whis-pered prayer; ev - 'ry need and ev - 'ry care.

Ask of Me, and I will give. Ask of Me, and

you will live. Ask of Me. Ask_____ of

24

NARRATION:

Jesus's ministry grew in fame, and people were following Him wherever He went. Eventually, His journey led Him to the great city of Jerusalem. As He drew near the city, He began to weep. "Jerusalem, Jerusalem, how often would I have gathered your children as a hen gathers her brood under her wings yet you were not willing." Soon, He would enter the city in a great parade of praise. The crowds would take palm branches and go out to Him shouting, "Hosanna! Blessed is He who comes in the name of the Lord."
(Matthew 21:9; 23:37, 39 paraphrased)

PALM BRANCHES

Words by
J. PAUL WILLIAMS (ASCAP)

Music by
DOUGLAS NOLAN (BMI)

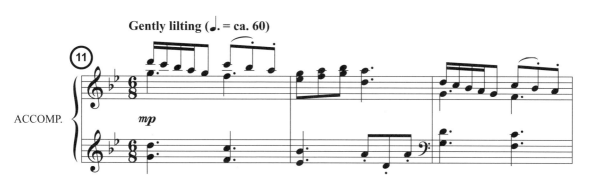

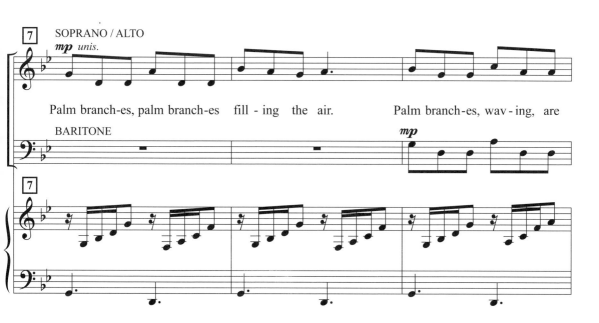

A GATHERING OF GRACE - SA(T)B

28

32

Palm branch - es, palm branch - es
laid at the feet of the King.
laid at the feet of the King.
Sing ho - san - na.
Sing ho - san - na.

NARRATION:

Following His triumphant entry into Jerusalem, Jesus began to look ahead to the time of Passover. In His heart, He knew that this was the last time He would celebrate this important moment with His disciples. Following His instructions, the disciples were led to a large upper room where they all gathered for the sacred meal. During this time of fellowship and worship, Jesus revealed more fully His mission of grace. From that upper room, God's divine light shone with golden promise and the world would never be the same.

A LIGHT IN THE UPPER ROOM

Words and Music by
DOUGLAS NOLAN (BMI)

can - dle of hope is burn - ing in the night. There's a

light in the up - per room._____ There's a light in the up - per

room. There's a place in the up - per

In the

36

38

hope and love. There's a song in the up - per room. There's a

song in the up - per room. There's a

light in the up - per room.

NARRATION:

Then Jesus went with His disciples to a place called Gethsemane, and He said to them, "Stay here, while I go over there and pray." Jesus was overwhelmed with sorrow and He fell to the ground and prayed, saying, "My Father, if it be possible, let this cup pass from Me; nevertheless, not as I will, but as You will." There, in that shadowed garden, Jesus embraced His destiny and found peace and strength to complete the work of grace.

(Matthew 26:36-39 paraphrased)

JESUS, IN GETHSEMANE

Words by
J. PAUL WILLIAMS (ASCAP)

Music by
DOUGLAS NOLAN (BMI)

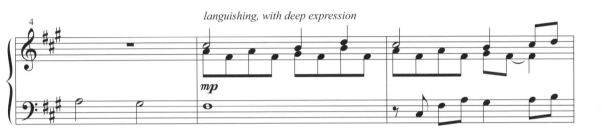

42

praying 'neath the olive trees, falling there on bended knee, crying out in agony. Our Lord, in deepest grief, filled with hu-

A GATHERING OF GRACE - SA(T)B

There, in that qui-et place,

He felt death's cold em-brace and lift-ed

high the cup of grace.

46

55
mf
There, in - side the gar - den wall, as the night be -
gins to fall, God's Son sur - ren - ders all for
love.
mp (opt. solo)
Fa - ther, let Thy
58
61
23
63

48

NARRATION:

In Gethsemane, a large crowd armed with swords and clubs confronted Jesus. Soldiers arrested Jesus and took Him away to face the Roman authorities. Jesus was violently beaten and given over to be crucified. Jesus was taken into the Praetorium, and a whole company of soldiers gathered around Him. They struck Him and adorned Him with a scarlet robe. They twisted together a crown of thorns and set it upon His head. They put a staff in His right hand and knelt in front of Him crying, "HAIL THE KING OF THE JEWS!" They spit upon Him and struck Him on the head repeatedly. Then, they led Him away to be crucified. When they had come to the place called Golgotha, He was fastened to a cross and raised high into the darkening Judean sky. In that moment, the words of Isaiah were made complete: "He was pierced for our transgressions, He was crushed for our iniquities; the punishment that brought us peace was upon Him and by His wounds we are healed." *(Matthew 27:29-33; Isaiah 53:5 KJV)*

THE DAY THE CROSS HELD UP THE SKY

Words and Music by
DOUGLAS NOLAN (BMI)

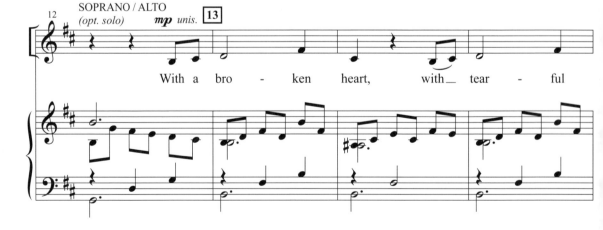

With a bro - ken heart, with tear - ful

eyes, the __ Sav - ior stands con - demned to die. Can we know the pain He felt in - side on the lone - ly day the cross held up the sky?

(end solo)

32 · SOPRANO / ALTO · ㉕

BARITONE

mf

At the

32

36 · *p*

Oo _____ oo _____

sound of wood, at the bird's first cry, the ___

36 · *mf*

40 · *mf* *unis.*

oo _____

See the

cross is lift - ed up on high.

40

54

N

57

A GATHERING OF GRACE - SA(T)B

maz - ing, so di - vine, on the

lone - ly day the cross held up the

sky._____ Oo_____

NARRATION:

And so we wait for the coming of dawn. We wait, holding on to hope, reaching into the night for some fragile flicker of sacred flame to assure us. We wait in the stillness, considering our place in this profound moment. And, with broken hearts, we see our reflections in the wine, our hands on the spear that pierced Him and the thorns of each sin that bruised His brow. Here, in the shadow of Calvary's cross, we wait and weep and give ourselves to grace. For through grace, we mourn this darkness not as people without hope, but as people who know and love the light.

A GREEN HILL FAR AWAY

Words by
CECIL FRANCES ALEXANDER (1818-1895)

Music by
DOUGLAS NOLAN (BMI)

fail-ing love, fol-low Him and try His works to do.

He died that we might be for-giv'n. He

He a-lone could un-lock the gate of___ heav'n and let us

in.___ There is a

green hill far a-way, out-side a cit-y wall, where__

Christ, the Lord, was cru-ci-fied, Who died to save us all. We may not

know, we can-not tell what pains He had to bear; but

we be-lieve it was for us He hung and suf-fered

68

A GATHERING OF GRACE - SA(T)B

PRAYER: *Optional*

God, grant us, in this moment, both sorrow and hope. Gift us with tears of remorse and the deep peace of true repentance. Grant us faith for this journey of remembrance, so that we might arrive in the garden restored, renewed, and ready…ready to embrace new life, ready to rise and roll our stones away… ready to receive our gift of alleluia!

RECESSIONAL

Music by
DOUGLAS NOLAN (BMI)

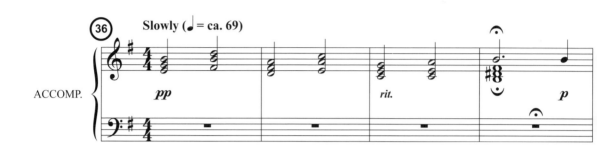

ACCOMP.

72